Modern Scottish Painters
NUMBER EIGHT

William Johnstone

by Douglas Hall, for the University Press
Edinburgh

© Edinburgh University Press, 1980
22 George Square, Edinburgh
with the financial support of the
Scottish Arts Council

ISBN 0 85224 385 5

Set by Speedspools, Edinburgh, and
printed in Great Britain by
Ivanhoe Printing Co, Edinburgh

Preface

This book has been made possible by two people, and one circumstance. The people are William Johnstone himself and his wife Mary. The circumstance is the existence of a large body of typescript transcribed from tapes dictated by William Johnstone, and now formed into an autobiography as yet unpublished. On the practical side of assembling the information for this book, and generally conducting a fifteen-year-old friendship with the Johnstone family, I owe everything to Mary Johnstone for her infinite hospitality and remarkable powers of organisation. Many years younger than her husband, she has presided over and made possible his full and productive life since his retirement, with the strong support of their daughter Sarah. As the advance of years has taken its toll of William's memory, Mary Johnstone has been there to clarify the facts and to provide a different perspective, often, on his conclusions. Her reticence about her own art as an embroiderer has gone beyond modesty.

The existence of the transcripts (which William was beginning when I first knew him well, and in which I played a small part in early days) might seem to make writing this book an easy task. Actually this has not been so. They have made it possible and they may partly account for the structure of this book, which is more biographical than critical. They have not made it easy. It must be admitted that William Johnstone is a difficult subject for study. There is something of the magician about him, and his constructs are not always capable of sober assessment. I have explained once or twice in the text what that means in practice. I have had to consider the difficult question of the sources of William's style, on which his autobiography is almost silent, and I am conscious of giving only fragmentary answers to the questions, all-important to the art-historian: Where does it come from? How original is it? How does it fit into context? The pursuit of those questions may easily become an irritant to the subject and to the layman, and another occasion will have to be found for them. My hope, in this book, is to have produced an outline of a creative personality not so much by direct portraiture but by tracing the influences that moulded it and the events that formed it.

In addition to the artist and his wife and daughter I owe thanks to the few people in Scotland with whom I shared, at first, an interest in William's work, such as Cordelia and George Oliver and Martin Baillie; to Mrs Hope Scott whose unfailing enthusiasm for the work often refreshed me; to Ronald (Micky) Marshall of the Stone Gallery in Newcastle, who first introduced me to William; and to the late McNeill Reid, who first took me to Satchells Farm. Victor Pasmore, William Turnbull, Hans Tisdall, Morris Kestelman, Nigel Walters and Theo Crosby have helped me on the subject of William's teaching years. Apart from my own introduction in the catalogue of the retrospective exhibition of 1970,

Tamara Krikorian and John McEwen have been the first in recent years to approach his work in a critical and historical way.

Finally I am grateful to the Edinburgh University Press for their forbearance in the matter of the timing of this book, which has been for me a strictly spare-time occupation.

DOUGLAS HALL
Edinburgh, July 1979

Publisher's Note. The publication of these monographs came about at the instigation of the Scottish Arts Council, which felt that, apart from sporadic articles and features in the press, art journals and exhibition catalogues, there was a dearth of critical and biographical material on contemporary Scottish artists. These books are, therefore, an attempt to provide well illustrated, critical and expository studies, which will not only communicate the peculiar excellence of each artist but also analyse their work in the light of twentieth-century Scottish painting, and indeed in the wider context of European art as a whole. In this way it is hoped to promote a wider acquaintance with the work of those artists and, perhaps most importantly, to stimulate the reader, who has not already had either the inclination or the opportunity, to look at the actual paintings.

The publishers have made every effort to establish and locate the owners of paintings illustrated, and apologise to those concerned when this has proved impossible. They will be glad to receive notification of up-to-date information on this matter for any future editions of the books.

William Johnstone [signature]

I AM DRIVING down the A68 from Edinburgh to-wards Jedburgh on a day in early February after a harsh January. The atmosphere is thin and sour with the faintest line of pinkish light breaking at the horizon like the early beginnings of a smile. The snow is slow to go from the long upland fields toiling up to dark opacities of woods on the distant scarp. Where heavy ploughland is set just so to the abrasive wind a marvellous spare pattern of rich brown lines has appeared through the dusty white. Looking at one such visual episode I am suddenly reminded that at the end of many a journey of mine along that road lies the hospitable house of William Johnstone and a sheaf of drawings I have perhaps not seen before yet, in another sense, have always known. Through the windscreen, I am looking at a William Johnstone. It is a brush drawing imbued with a Chinese fatalism, where the dark liquid depth of a broad horizontal stroke on the white paper – the wood – and the thin strong vertical lines of the pen – the dykes and fences – evoke instantly the spare, gaunt, abstract landscape as I see it now.

I am looking at a photograph full of period charm and antiquarian and aesthetic interest [p.84]. It shows a great perspective of a border field under sowing, some time before the First World War. The huge expanse of upland ground – so lonely in our present minds' eye – is here a stage for a disciplined and purposeful movement of men, horses, and – oh joy – machines, directed by a figure in the middle distance who is identified as the father of William Johnstone. Nearer to the camera is William himself, a diminutive and stocky figure in whom can be seen already the humour and pertinacity, the deter-mination to be where the action is, that characterise him today. Greenhead Farm, Selkirk, where the photograph was taken about 1909, lies somewhat to the west of the Jedburgh road, in similar country. Perhaps the land-scape is a little more rounded in contour there, as it be-comes when one moves west and south into the wilder-ness of whalebacked hills in Dumfriesshire, the unruly Western Marches of former times, and on down to the 'debatable lands' around the Solway Firth. In those countries Johnstones of old waged their murderous war-fare during the lawlessness of the Border, occasionally against the English, more often against other families like the Armstrongs and Maxwells with whom they dis-puted the leadership of the Western March. Like other Border people, William's family had considerable pride of race, and place.

William Johnstone, the painter's father, came to Greenhead Farm, high above Selkirk, in 1902 – William was then four or five years old. There began one of the most absorbing childhoods a boy could have. The bigger farms of Edwardian Britain were the finest development of a system that evolved over more than a century, and has disappeared for ever. Harsh though the work was, and unequal the rewards, the richness of the ecology and the balance of the system, the life it sustained from a given amount of land, raised it to a very considerable achievement of civilisation. For an impressionable and thoughtful boy, to grow up in such a system meant, besides good food and security, an early appreciation of fundamentals: of birth and death, and the realisation that death is essential to life; of cause and effect, the exact relation of reward to effort; of relentless responsibility for life; of functionalism, and the use of power; of the final dependence of everything on the land. No wonder that when William finally reached the Edinburgh College of Art, he found himself both at a disadvantage with his fellow students and at the same time far more mature. Knowledge of fundamentals like these is not necessarily liberating, but may rather be suffocating. Once realised it may suggest escape, as from a trap.

Meanwhile, for the young boy and the adolescent, life was very good. As it was William Johnstone living it, it was also lived intensely. Those solid Scottish farmhouses, so grey to outward appearances, housed a famous, abundant hospitality, much company and coming and going of relatives and friends. Often they housed large families, but at Greenhead this was not so. The Johnstones had two other children, daughters who were older than William. One died when he was only four, giving him his first indelible impression of mystery and suffering. He was a highly impressionable child. Another event that profoundly affected him was the death by drowning of one of the farm children. For William these events were one and the same kind with his experience with his animals. More intense maybe, they aroused the same emotions as the death of animals he loved. There was a dog his father had had shot. This posed the child with the sort of emotional problems most people try to escape from all their lives. With part of him he knew his father was right but he could not help seeing the shooting as a cowardly betrayal. William remembers this incident vividly and perhaps it was a small factor in the big decision he had to make later. Be that as it may, those days produced in him the fanatical reverence that he has always had for life, and his hatred of any sort of cruelty and destruction.

As an only son, William became his father's partner, assistant and prop at a ridiculously young age. This too signalled conflict – conflict between duty to his father and the farm, and duty to be educated; more basically, a tug-of-war between present life outside and deferred life in school. Life was very real for him when he found himself at the age of twelve having to herd animals many miles back from market with darkness falling, or drive his incapable father back from a neighbouring town in the trap. Up to a point, the law solved this particular conflict, and William had to attend Knowe Park school like all the other Selkirk children, except that he had the walk of several miles each way in all weathers. William was the sort of child that British education has always found most difficult to cope with – acutely intelligent, creative, practical and non-academic. Given this and his divided loyalties, his Scottish teachers seem to have coped remarkably well, and he remembers them with respect. It was not until he reached the High School at age of fourteen that real strains began to develop.

The Greenwoods, William's mother's family, were textile people from Lancashire and Hawick. They were an extensive family, who were richer and more cosmopolitan than the farming people on his father's side. William eagerly responded to this – he was impressionable, loved to be dazzled and to admire. He eagerly lapped up every report of the wider world. The Greenwoods also stood for something akin to art, they understood the importance of colour, pattern and texture and actually employed fortunate people to work with these entrancing qualities. William's mother had been to art galleries as a child, and her father, Robert Greenwood, was one of the founders of the Art Gallery in Hawick. Influences like that were leaven at Greenhead Farm. When William wanted a paint-box it was his mother he cajoled to buy it, and in her mild and gentle way she encouraged his first efforts to use it. Johnstone senior seems to have been predictably indifferent to William's first efforts at painting. He did not realise that they began a process that would eventually drive his son away from farming. Not that he contributed nothing to his son's artistic education. By letting William have responsi-bilities beyond his years for machinery and animals alike, he may have thought he was rivetting the youngster to his profession. What he actually did was to give him the most deeply impressed visual and tactile memories of these things which, with their respective powers of man-directed and natural function, lie at the very basis of art. William was madly interested in his paint-box and what he could make it do. His first successful original painting was of his collie dog, Rock [3].

William's beginnings in the business of art were sound. Every year Bibby's Cattle-Cake Calendar arrived at the farm – not pin-ups or rose-girt cottages but excellent colour reproductions of old master paintings. William was carried away by the beauty of these, so what more natural than for him to copy them. The reproductions in the calendar taught him the vital transition from seeing pictorially. But he stumbled on another vital truth, or rather his nature presented no other possibility to him: *Painting was something you did with paint.* Every visual sensation had to be *translated* into paint. He had no use for reproductions in his calendars that did not look like paintings. The Pre-Raphaelites meant nothing to him; he could not see how they were done. In his own words 'I could do nothing with Holman Hunt because the illustration superseded the qualities of the medium'. William never lost this salutary attitude to paint. He also continued to copy for many years, but always constructively. Compared with copying, painting from nature and especially landscape was a deeply disappointing and frustrating business for the boy. Fortunately

4 [1]

there was no-one at hand to tell him that copying was an inferior activity or that only direct painting from nature was art.

One of William's childhood copies has survived – not from Bibby's calendar but from a humbler model like a Christmas card [1]. For all that the subject is hackneyed, the little painting must rank as an original in its painterly translation of the visual effect, and it shows considerable competence in handling the breadth of light on the surface of the river and its recession, which are recorded more vividly, one may be certain, than in the model copied. The other very early painting we have is from nature, but not from landscape. William's sheepdog, Rock, was very dear to his heart. At first the small painting, now rather grimy, is not particularly interesting, until you consider that from the dot of light on his wet nose to the tuft at the end of his tail he is observed and conceived purely in the difficult and adult medium of oil paint. To look at a detail of Rock's upstanding collar of white hairs [2] is to see a classic piece of painterly translation which the painter today acknowledges as in every way worthy of himself.

This painting of Rock was made just about the time of the first 'crisis' of William's life. In 1911 he and his parents had to decide whether they wanted him to go on to receive what could then fairly be called an 'academic' education. They were advised he was capable of it, as he obviously was, so William started at Selkirk High School. It was not art that brought the experiment to an end the following year. William at fourteen was already a farmer.

By 1911 there was an up-turn in agriculture. Johnstone senior was beginning to prosper greatly, and had more need of his son than ever. William loved his responsibilities and even the tremendous work involved. And the teaching at Selkirk was more academic than he had dreamed of. Never submissive and always creative, he lapsed into lethargy or produced affronts to the system as when, called on to recite *The Lay of the Last Minstrel*, he produced an impromptu parody in Scots and was ejected from the room. William was already rebelling not so much against learning, which he respected and wished for himself, but against lifeless irrelevance and (in the case just mentioned) against Anglified values in the teaching. His father would not have taken him from school for purely selfish reasons but, as William was already languishing, the conclusion seemed obvious. So William left Selkirk High School in 1912.

Although William was now a full-time farmer, his interest in art did not by any means disappear. There was not much art in the Borders, but there was one artist of great merit whose story illustrates too well what tends to happen to an artist in that kind of society. Tom Scott (1854–1927) was a draughtsman of real gifts, who had a small but distinctive originality of vision. Constantly under pressure to reduce his work to a formula, monopolised by a few patrons, with few contacts with art in the wide world, although he was an RSA, he finished up a drunkard and a 'character'. It was in that phase of his life that William was sent to him, and began to go on expeditions with him to paint and to look for flints and things of interest. Tom Scott was a disillusioned man, and when William began to confide in him some thoughts of being a professional artist, and going to study art in Edinburgh, he made no attempt to hide his misgivings. To be an artist, he said, was a gamble with life itself, was loneliness and unremitting work, with the near certainty of eventual compromise and failure. He had little time for the people in Edinburgh: William would very likely learn more from his fellow students than his teachers – but he would do better to stay an amateur. However, he was prepared to say William had more talent than others who had consulted him. . . . Tom Scott was to keep up with the young painter until near his death in 1927. Always his message was the same: work, observe, study, do not be deflected. If he did nothing else for William, he succeeded in imbuing him with the most serious respect for a painter's vocation, something that few of his fellow-countrymen could distinguish in its own right, as a thing apart from commercial success.

Perhaps if it had not been for the First World War, William would have taken Tom Scott's advice and remained an amateur painter and a farmer. As it was, the outbreak of war in his eighteenth year threw him into the work of the farm in deadly earnest. His father was ageing; but suddenly an enormous effort was required of British agriculture, while the men who had staffed the farms so lavishly began to be drained off to die in the trenches. As William's military age and universal conscription approached his father got him reserved. but as the ghastly trawl of men went wider and deeper, William was at last sucked in. He was conscripted in spring 1918, just in time to feel the tremors of a terrible breakdown that might have come near to convulsing the British army and so changing the course of history if the Armistice had not been concluded in time. William was and is acutely sensitive to atmosphere. From his worm's eye view as a new recruit he could see that the army was almost demoralised. This terrible sensation, not actual experience of bloodshed, gave William a profound anti-militarism. He was fortunate enough never to reach the trenches. Immediately before the armistice he was

detached from his unit and transferred to the Labour Corps, and found himself posted to agricultural work – at Greenhead Farm. He has brilliantly evoked the mingled relief and anti-climax that he felt on trudging up the hill to the farm where his parents, caught by surprise, greeted him almost with shyness. It was November 11, 1918. In truth, something had changed in these people and in the world and the old relationship could not be resumed.

The next year was to present the second crisis in the life of William Johnstone. His father was tired out and wished to retire. His ambition was to see his son take over the farm he had built up. He was ready to discuss financial arrangements. His whole existence was bound up in this idea of continuity. Without any pretensions to gentle rank, he had a stubborn pride in the calling of the farmer and a fierce independence that seems both touching and admirable. It was almost inconceivable to him that his son should reject his inheritance to follow the frivolous, risky occupation of artist, and when he had to conceive of it, he found it a bitter blow. For William it was also a cruel dilemma. Yet his mind was soon made up, and then everything was settled rapidly. Greenhead Farm was sold up in May 1919, to the sombre disapproval of their Border neighbours. Thirty years later, when William was again becoming a familiar figure in the region, there were those who had not forgiven him. His parents moved to a villa in Selkirk, and William spent the summer unhappily fencing in Yarrow.

In October 1919 Johnstone started at the Edinburgh College of Art. He was twenty-two, older than the pre-war average, and certainly wiser. So began his first acquaintance with the Edinburgh art scene. It was not encouraging to him. Of all the staff at the College, he remembers only one with respect and gratitude: Henry Lintott (1877–1965). Lintott, an academician and a painter of rather fey allegories as well as some poetic landscapes, was not the sort of figure one would expect to appeal to Johnstone, or Johnstone to him. But among some very narrow and bigoted teachers, who thought only of imitation, Lintott was one who allowed the possibility, even the primacy, of *thinking*. His criticism was severe and sardonic, but thoughtful. He also was more experienced and cosmopolitan than many of the staff. Johnstone was drawn to this Englishman. Lintott encouraged him when he would otherwise have concluded that, if what was taught at Edinburgh was art, then what he had dreamt of since childhood must be something else. In a sense he was right. The problem was to find a source and a confirmation of his own kind of art. Lintott was no modernist; he belonged to the age of Ricketts and Shannon. But his influence can be seen in one or two surviving paintings by Johnstone from his art-school days.

In spite of his disillusion with the teaching, Johnstone's college years were not barren. At Tom Scott's suggestion, he went to Amsterdam to study Rembrandt and Frans Hals. At this time he met a cousin, the composer Francis George Scott, and also C.M. Grieve

(Hugh MacDiarmid) with whom he kept up an acquaintance based on mutual respect until MacDiarmid's death in 1978. For a time the three of them formed a group. They were united by at least one thing – a hatred of the cultural poverty of Scotland and her helot relationship to England. This was to be the fuel that drove Mac-Diarmid until the end of his life – not a sour hatred of the English as has been supposed. Johnstone's attitude to these problems was certainly not so radical, for he was not a politicised individual like MacDiarmid. He followed his career to England and in some measure adopted English ways, but there were aspects of the English manner of doing things which he never accepted, and this dissidence of his within English governing society was an important factor in the way his career developed. As a painter he never drew much from current English art, finding his sources of inspiration rather in Europe and America.

Johnstone painted two portraits of Francis George Scott [16] and several of MacDiarmid at various times. MacDiarmid knew nothing of painting, but supported Johnstone in pugnacious fashion with high claims, for he knew him to be dissident, highly individual and in no-one's pocket. These were sufficient claims to support as far as MacDiarmid was concerned, for they stood for truth to oneself, a mind free from the tricks of the trade, and a personality resistant to promotion by the pundits or the media. However, the finest tribute that MacDiarmid paid to Johnstone was not in any polemical catalogue introduction, but in those occasions when the poet laid his great gifts alongside the painter's to serve the same ends of expression; of what, they perhaps hardly knew, only its immensity:

How the boundless dwells perfect and undivided in
    the spirit,
How each part can be infinitely great and infinitely
    small,
How the utmost extension is but a point, and how
Light, harmony, movement, power
All identical, all separate, and all united are life.

Francis George Scott was a very different character. He had actually taught MacDiarmid at Langholm Academy, and recognised the quality of the poetry he was writing after his return from the war. Francis George Scott's dissidence had a different timbre from MacDiarmid's; lacking the underlying and enduring political base, it was more effervescent and, perhaps, more hedonistic. He had studied literature under the great George Saintsbury and had been nominated for the Tait Poetry Prize, but music had intervened and he had eventually graduated in music from Durham while teaching at Langholm. He could introduce Johnstone to worlds he hardly yet knew, and his powerful, somewhat arrogant personality made him for a time the leader of this little group of three. To the vulgarity and sentiment of Scottish art and manners he opposed only disdain, which rendered his effort to renew Scottish music from within impossibly difficult. Of the three, Francis George Scott's and William Johnstone's tasks were the more difficult, as they had less than MacDiarmid that was truly native, on which to build. Their disparities, especially MacDiarmid's politics and Scott's a-political nationalism, forced the group apart. Scott's work never gained wide currency and he is only now being re-evaluated. But for a time the group was a real stimulus. Fortunately, Johnstone was more inclined to Mac-Diarmid's view, not of politics, but of life in street, market-place and wherever it is lived. Hating real vulgarity and meanness, Johnstone was well able to enjoy the absurdities of music-hall and touring theatre (he once played super to Sir Frank Benson, and forgot his lines) and like MacDiarmid has enjoyed the battle all his life.

Another stimulus during the Edinburgh years was the lecture course given by the Professor of Fine Art, G. Baldwin Brown. His lectures were regarded as a joke by many students, but they set Johnstone on a path of thought that was to influence his whole development. Baldwin Brown was an authority on Celtic, Saxon and Romanesque art, and his lectures, although wide-ranging, did not satisfy the student urge to hear about their own day. Edinburgh, in short, did not realise the reputation of its Professor. Johnstone had far more than the usual student's degree of intellectual curiosity and omnivorous appetite for visual experience; even so the full relevance of Baldwin Brown's teaching did not strike him until a few years later, when he was desperately searching for his own true artistic heritage. It was the example of Baldwin Brown that taught him to apply the long view to the problem of contemporary art, as Johnstone tried to do in his book *Creative Art in Britain*.

While at Edinburgh College of Art Johnstone met an American student who had come, rather improbably, to study sculpture, having heard that one of the staff, Alexander Carrick (d. 1966) was the man to teach direct carving. She had already been in Paris and was familiar with the ideas of modern art. Flora Macdonald, from her romantic expatriate name through her outstanding looks [*14*] to her cosmopolitan knowledge of foreign places and exciting ideas and her American participatory vitality, was immensely attractive to the equally vital but still raw Scots student. But Flora and William did not immediately throw in their lot together. Flora, having learned what she could from Alexander Carrick, returned to Paris. Johnstone received his DA from Edinburgh in 1923, but remained for an extra year of drawing there and at the RSA. He was plainly not an ingratiating student, but one who would tend to divide the opinion of the staff, or divide the outside examiner from the head of department as happened, it is said, when Johnstone was pitted against W. G. Gillies for the travelling scholarship. Johnstone did not win the travelling scholarship from the College, but in 1924 the RSA awarded him three prizes, and in 1925 a Carnegie Travelling Scholarship. It was characteristic of Johnstone that he should have rolled the McLean Watters Medal along the aisle during the presentation ceremony, thereby putting his Scholarship at risk. But he was awarded it, and there seems to have been no doubt in his mind what he should do with it. In choosing to go to Paris, Johnstone might seem to have shown less than his usual originality. But originality at that point would have done him no good. Paris was still the centre of ideas in art, and no Scotsman had yet come to terms with what it had to offer, although many had preceded him there. In the cold autumn of 1925, Johnstone set off for Paris.

Artists' travels always have some of the paradoxical nature noted by G.K. Chesterton who, found packing his bags at home in Battersea and asked where he was going, said 'Battersea'. In other words, artists travel also to discover themselves and their roots. Johnstone was certainly intensely conscious of his own roots, which he had forcibly pulled out of the Border land. Thanks to Tom Scott, and Baldwin Brown, he was realising that there were visible traces of something infinitely older than the Victorian ethos he had inherited. But he was a long way yet from being able to use it as the basis of any work of his. This is an appropriate moment to see what he had achieved in terms of painting. Although he has destroyed so much, something has prompted Johnstone to keep some of these youthful works through all the vicissitudes of his later life.

One of these is *Potato-diggers, Millerhill* [*4*], which Johnstone submitted for his Diploma in 1923. It is easy to understand why Sir George Clausen, the external examiner that year, liked the picture. Its subject is close to his own pictures of farm-workers (Sir George Clausen, RA 1852–1944, painter and writer on art, was one of the few British practitioners of the rural social realism fathered by Millet). It is also easy to understand why Johnstone, of all art students, should have chosen the subject, and why Clausen, predicting a fine career for him, might probably have foreseen an entirely different course to the one he followed. Johnstone painted *Potato-diggers* from drawings he had made the previous November (1922). The potato-fields were among the nearest he could find to the city, in the flat fertile but now half industrialised tract between Musselburgh and Dalkeith. The women were the 'tattie-howkers', travelling bands of Irish and others, mostly women, who did this back-breaking, seasonal work. Johnstone had known all about itinerant farm workers in his farming days – he knew their character, their incredible endurance, their habits and the impossibility of their breaking out of the system of which they formed a part. This knowledge informs the painting, which also shows great formal qualities, without which realism cannot be strong enough to enforce its message on the reluctant eye. The painting of the two main figures, though the right-hand one is awkward, has the clumsiness of strength and potential growth, not of incompetence. There is a strong sense of abstract form in the way the heads and backs are grouped together, already foreshadowing his future development. The delicacy of the landscape running back to the blue line of the Firth of Forth contrasts with the harshness of the foreground and proclaims a debt to the generalised symbolism of the late nineteenth century in its nicely judged two-dimensional structure and aerial perspective.

12 [4]

Potato-diggers is rather an enigma. Already impressive, and promising still more, growing out of his whole experience, it seems to be a completely isolated work. The drawings for it do not survive and there are no other drawings of this kind. Maybe this was one of Johnstone's characteristic rejections. He had escaped from farming; he was not going to become a chronicler of labour and fill sketchbooks with drawings of workers or farm animals. However, if it was inevitable for Johnstone to reject realism in order to be of his time, it was not so easy to renounce the landscape itself. The landscape remains the basis of his whole evolution. There is a photograph of a small landscape, now lost or destroyed, which was painted at about this time [5]. It represents the country just beyond his father's villa in Selkirk. This was painted for Johnstone's own satisfaction. The decisive, even harsh way in which the rising landscape has been schematised, the impatient shorthand for trees and buildings, may have been confined in those days to pictures he painted for himself. But they were typical of him and were not to be concealed for long. When this painting was done, Johnstone can have seen almost nothing of modern painting. Cézanne was still regarded with suspicion by most of the staff at Edinburgh in 1924, and Braque's fifteen-year-old cubist paintings regarded as the works of a dangerous revolutionary or a charlatan. So the bold conception of the *motif* in Johnstone's picture, which owes something to both these masters, is highly original. The fidelity underlying this schematic way of painting brings the border scene to instant life.

Such observation within conceptualisation continued to be a mark of Johnstone's art all his life.

On the evidence of this and other paintings (although dates are hard to establish) one would say that Johnstone was well prepared for the introduction to modern, conceptualised art that he would receive in Paris. Scottish students seem often to have gone to Paris as a not very serious interval in the process of establishing themselves at home; some perhaps went to have their prejudices confirmed. Johnstone went in a different spirit, as a man who had burned his boats and did not know what the future held for him. He was conscious of a revulsion against much that he was leaving behind, the system from which he felt that he was escaping. The trouble was to find an alternative. The fields of Northern France were visibly the scene of the same harsh law of labour as his own had been. Arrived in Paris, the loneliness of his position as a young provincial without French struck him with its inevitable force. He had made no plans, so he did what many had done before him and attended one of the open drawing schools, the Grande Chaumière, where a model without instruction was provided. These affairs were a lottery – they could be intolerably rowdy, but one might find oneself next to a future star of the Ecole de Paris. As well as this, Johnstone wanted to find a master. He went to see Amedée Ozenfant, the 'Purist' painter, Fernand Léger, who wanted to take him as a farmer's son like himself, and André Lhote. Surprisingly, Johnstone chose Lhote, as had many other students from Edinburgh. But he never regretted his choice.

André Lhote (1885–1962) was a fine artist, although no-one has ever been over-excited by his paintings. He was engaged in codifying the discoveries of more volatile masters who, themselves, had moved on to something else. This systematic approach made him a good teacher, and he was a severe one, a grammarian of painting. He taught from direct study of the model combined with study of past masterpieces. Analysis of a large reproduction of a Rembrandt hanging on the wall would be compared to that of the model he had set up. Lhote was not interested in detailed imitation; students were required to analyse the appearance of the model in terms of areas of light and dark and of coolness and warmth. The student's job was to analyse in order to synthesise, and Lhote saw to it that in setting up his models – not always living ones – the most disparate and unrelated things were sometimes offered as a challenge to the student's unifying powers. Unity extended also to the whole sheet, and formal analysis had to embrace the running out of the subject to the edges. In every way, then, Lhote was concerned with making pictures – pictorial wholes, not studies. Contrary to what has sometimes been inferred about Lhote, Johnstone did not find his teaching in the least stultifying. On the contrary, it was flexible and did not lose sight of humanity.

As Lhote himself stressed, one did not learn to paint by sitting in the studio. That was particularly true in Paris, where artists of so many nationalities, young geniuses and dullards alike, were coming together to try to find some common elixir – an alchemical artistic preparation with which pavement and café tables were supposed to be covered. What happened, if they were lucky, was that they found each other, themselves, and their own traditions. British students were usually at a disadvantage in this process, lumbered with national shyness, poor communicators, and above all uncertain of their own visual culture. This was certainly no less true of the Scots among them. But it was impossible for a young man of Johnstone's temperament and consuming interest in everything to remain in Paris and get nothing out of it. His vivid recall brings a fellow-student at the Grande Chaumière to life – a farouche, tousled, depressive young man who drew by fits and starts, scattering drawings on the floor, always dissatisfied with the model and seeking to find in it something that corresponded to his inner conception of forms in space. Probably Johnstone never actually spoke to Alberto Giacometti, who became one of the most famous sculptors of the age. The latter addressed anyone who would listen, and few did, for he was generally thought to be mad. Oddly enough it was another sculptor who, in retrospect, spoke to Johnstone in the voice, so to speak, of his whole Paris experience: the Spaniard, Julio Gonzalez, twenty-one years his senior. They became in a distant way friends, and Gonzalez called on Johnstone in later days in London. Gonzalez (1876–1942) was typical of those who found their whole background – in his case that of Spanish metalworking – transmuted by the Paris experience of which his compatriot Picasso formed for him an overwhelming part. Gonzalez was just then

embarking on his career as a free fabricator of metal sculpture that brought him, if only posthumously, a fame little less than Giacometti's. Gonzalez's message echoed that of Francis George Scott and perhaps aroused memories of Baldwin Brown. Cleverness was not enough. It needed an outlet worthy of it. But nationalism was not enough either; it needed a vocabulary, and all had to be fused into the peculiar consciousness of our time.

Johnstone might never have got beyond these studio encounters. In a sense, he never did. Shyness and that deep-rooted spirit of independence amounting to automatic rejection of everything offered to him, prevented him from knocking on many doors that might have opened to him. No lion-hunter, he never sought out the powerful or famous, and least of all the fashionable. But he did, of course, have a life outside the studios. An American, Max Bernd-Cohen, became his close companion. Max, a law graduate of Columbia, was looking at life and considering whether to become a painter. William became his artistic and professional mentor, and together they went round the galleries and tried to assess and understand the new painting. In return Max contributed his extrovert nature, his cosmopolitan background and experience of the world, and his better French. They went to the cafés where the artists and celebrities went, most often to the Dôme, where they saw, sometimes talked to, the big names – who were not then quite so big. They went to parties, to the races, and finally, in the spring of 1926, they decided to make a

journey. Johnstone wanted to make a copy in the Prado to take back to Edinburgh as evidence of his studies, so they set off for Madrid by routes that were, to say the least, devious, taking them by Carcassone to Barcelona where they got a tramp steamer to Tangier, back to Algeciras and to Seville in time for Holy Week. The little money they spent is inconceivable nowadays, but it was not done without running the gauntlet of barking fleas, which raised weals on Johnstone's legs, perils in unseaworthy boats and close shaves with Arabs and Spaniards. All this William recalls and relates with true picaresque *élan*. At Seville they remembered they were supposed to be artists and tried to hire a model, a mortifying process even with the help of a Spanish-speaking American Scot whom they had met on the journey. Eventually they persuaded a young Flamenco dancer (and her mother) to pose. They reached Madrid by way of Toledo where they were, for once, more conscious of the ancient dignity of Spain than the cruelty and poverty of the streets.

Johnstone set up his easel in the Prado, complete with piece of carpet to catch the drips. He had decided to copy Velasquez's *Aesop*. Something of the Edinburgh prejudices still lingered; remembering that Edinburgh valued *bravura* and associated Velasquez with Sargent, he dashed at it. Too late he thought of Lhote's teaching, retraced his steps and began to square up his design. As the days and weeks passed (he allowed himself a month for the job) he found in Velasquez first the precise geometrician and then Velasquez the great orchestrator of pigment and glazes. He learned the incredible difficulty in a great composition of relating the parts to the whole and, particularly, the edges to the centre, the thing that caused him the greatest number of false starts. He felt like a horseman fording a river, forced to commit himself to the current. Johnstone never forgot his experience of copying *Aesop*, which contributed to not only his skill as a painter but his education as a man. It forced him, impetuous and cocksure as he no doubt was, to recognise a master, *his* master. He deeply regrets that copying has dropped out of the education of artists.

Flora Macdonald, whom Johnstone had met in Edinburgh, was working in the sculpture class of Bourdelle, alongside Giacometti and Germaine Richier. Flora's presence in Paris coloured William's whole experience. Like Max Bernd-Cohen, Flora came from a much more cosmopolitan and adventurous background and had also been, at least until that time, wealthy. Her elderly relation, a Mrs Younger, kept an apartment and something of a 'salon' in Paris. Flora took William there once or twice. There he met Gertrude Stein, whom he hated, and her brother Leo, whom he liked and from whom he learned about Matisse. But Mrs Younger's society was smart and William, in his usual way, rejected any idea of profiting from 'lions' he might meet there. In this he had the backing of Flora herself. The scenario is clear and familiar – the wealthy girl rejecting the *moeurs* of her class, the young man from a different world, interested yet repelled by the world he was encountering through her, sensing the opportunity of escape from previous restrictions but fearful of stepping into others. So William and Flora made no killings at Mrs Younger's *salon*. On the other hand, Flora's family money seemed to promise independence. Flora and William decided to marry. She had enough, they thought, to keep them both until they had made names for themselves.

William Johnstone and Flora Macdonald were married at the British Consulate in Paris in the Spring of 1927. The years 1926–8 were critical ones for Johnstone's life and painting. He had not quite cut himself off emotionally from home, Selkirk and Scotland. He had to find the means to live, but above all he had to find a way to absorb the overwhelming effect of what he had seen and learned, and somehow graft it on to what he had already done and to his growing interest in his heritage. The chronology of that period has become a bit obscure. He seems to have paid a visit home in the summer of 1926, but probably did not spend long there, as he had nowhere to paint. He is convinced, however, that on that visit he produced a drawing [6], which is remarkably ahead of its time. His mother was ill, and he associates the drawing, done in his bedroom in a state of despondency and despair, with her illness. In 1925 the Surrealists, Joan Miró and particularly André Masson, had introduced the idea of 'automatic drawing', in which they tried to yield up the line to the promptings of the unconscious. Johnstone may well have heard of these experiments, but his own drawing is of a different

18 [6]

kind, being done with brush; it does not look to Masson but forward to Jackson Pollock. Hardly anywhere, in 1926, would such a drawing have been understood. In Selkirk it must have seemed to confirm the fears of Johnstone's parents that, as their aged servant put it, 'the young maister's back, and he's fair daft!' Probably Johnstone never let them see it. Finding his mother not in danger, he returned to Paris as quickly as he could.

However, marriage concentrates the mind wonderfully, especially of parents, and Flora was not to be concealed. Even so it is not quite clear why the pair returned to Selkirk very soon after they were married. They did, however, find somewhere to work – an ex-army hut belonging to the family doctor, Dr Graham. Mrs Graham was interested in art and a sound friend, but she thought that Johnstone should knuckle down to painting what people wanted, in the way that they wanted – she thought 'sincerity' could be taken too far. As for Dr Graham, he thought the young couple were quite mad, and told the father so. The latter had not quite given up hope that William would even yet go back to the land. He offered to buy him a certain farm with a nice house. But now he had Flora to contend with and she, although she could charm her father-in-law, had no intention of becoming a farmer's wife.

So William and Flora had a year of living in the villa and working together in the army hut. Flora was a competent and interesting artist. Her influence on Johnstone is impossible to estimate exactly now, but it was certainly great. She would have checked any tendency on his part to revert to insularity. From home she may have had word of the young school of modernism in America. Her energy and industry seem to have been outstanding. It was during that year, from the spring of 1927 to the spring of 1928, that Johnstone's art was forged from all that he had learned. Not only did he paint one or two pictures of outstanding interest then, but he laid up a stock, either of ideas, or of actual pictures begun, that carried him through all the lean years of teaching and struggling that followed, until he could devote himself to a new phase of his creative life. In those early years he began the practice that is the despair of those who would write about him, of taking up paintings after a lapse of years, and altering them according to his interests of that moment. Titles, too, might change and sometimes works have not been titled at all until recent years. Johnstone has also tried at various times in the last fifteen years to work out the chronology of his early, invariably undated work. Confident in the solution he found, he has applied dates to the back, but these have not always proved right.

These practices, which make things difficult for his chroniclers, stem from attitudes of mind that were also being forged in those early days. One difficulty is to know just what stage he had reached before going to Paris. We have already referred to the landscape behind Selkirk, which is in its way a very modern work. The picture now called *Celtic totem* [7], which is probably of 1925, before Paris, is not only modern but modernistic. It is an immature work, but contains many *motifs* that

20 [7]

would turn up again much later, and within its terms it functions well as a composition. The strong detached verticals against the predominantly diagonal grain of the landscape (echoed in all the little crosses on the left) do not accord with Lhote's teaching so that this is, little doubt, a pre-Paris painting substantially unaltered. In subject it is an odd, youthful mix of primitivist influences with a totemised 'Celtic' or more likely Saxon prince and princess (and their child?), against Border hills. Strangely, a buried head like an Easter Island statue also appears. Perhaps Johnstone identified with the child, for the tall figures do have, in relation to the landscape and the setting sun, a forbidding or a valedictory aspect. Maybe they are his parents and we should see the picture as a kind of voluntary expulsion from Paradise.

Sanctuary [8] may have started out as a similar, although more naturalistic kind of painting, also with strong verticals. But this one has certainly been altered to bring it into line with Lhotian principles. The figures are now quite successfully interlocked, and the distribution of light and dark passages gives volume, establishes profiles, and yet allows the eye to pass from one form to another. This last feature is the all-important idea of *passage* which Lhote and the cubists had taken from Cézanne. There are puzzling and unsatisfactory features in the painting as it stands today, such as the pale heads and the book to left and right, and the strange metallic cut-out one-dimensional white birds which cut a swathe with their sickle shapes across the left foreground. These seem to denote a third stage of alteration,

as they do not belong to the Lhote world of late cubism but to a new hard-edged abstraction that lay purely on the surface. The Johnstones were very interested in surfaces. They thought that they should bring in old techniques to redress the balance of the new, so they set about preparing panels with scrim, glue and gesso according to the processes analysed in A.P. Laurie's *The Painter's Methods and Materials*. They had bought a copy of this in Paris in 1926, the year of publication. Laurie was a professor at Heriot-Watt College and to illustrate his text he reproduced pictures in the National Galleries of Scotland. He also reproduced and praised the mural work of Phoebe Traquair, the artist of the Celtic revival, and described in detail the techniques of John Duncan RSA, another painter of this persuasion. The panels prepared by the Johnstones were most likely done according to Duncan's method described by Laurie. Phoebe Traquair and John Duncan would normally be considered the opposite pole to modernism, but as we have seen, Johnstone was not immune to the idea of Celtic revivalism. However, these panels were destined to be used by Flora for large decorative compositions, although William did make similar experiments for himself, including the use of gold on the prepared surface [13].

The best and most consistent painting of this period is *Folies Bergères* [9], which survives unaltered with its original title. This was Johnstone's trial of skill, owing to Paris its subject or starting-point (see the top left-hand corner) and its general type of structure, which is Lhotian in essence but rendered with heavy lines and an almost ponderous strength. The dancing-girls are almost wholly metamorphosed, but their lower limbs are as weighty as those of the travelling tattie-howkers a few years before. Indeed, it makes one realise how much the triangulated structure of *Potato-diggers* [4] already gets to the heart of the matter. *Folies Bergères* is also painted with an earthy palette appropriate to second-stage cubism if not to the subject, and has mellowed to an appearance of old-masterish authority. Its importance to Johnstone was as a synthesis of himself to date but, most importantly, it showed how he could extract from cubism the quite different rhythm he wanted, which was the principle he valued most in Celtic art. J.D. Fergusson had already been over some of this ground, but it is doubtful whether Johnstone knew his work at that date.

It was Fergusson who made the word 'rhythm' a catchword for the new art through his participation, as art editor, in the periodical of that name from 1911 to 1913, and the word has acquired a rather vague echo of modern Celticism. In Johnstone's case it was a serious matter to find somewhere in the Scottish tradition the wherewithal with which to build an original contribution to twentieth-century, non-naturalistic art. He thought to find it in Celtic art. Such sources are bound to be so much transmuted that it is difficult to be sure what they amounted to. Probably Johnstone did not draw a sharp distinction between Celtic, Pictish or Anglo-Saxon art. His main source of material was the carved stones and casts in the National Museum of Antiquities in Edin-

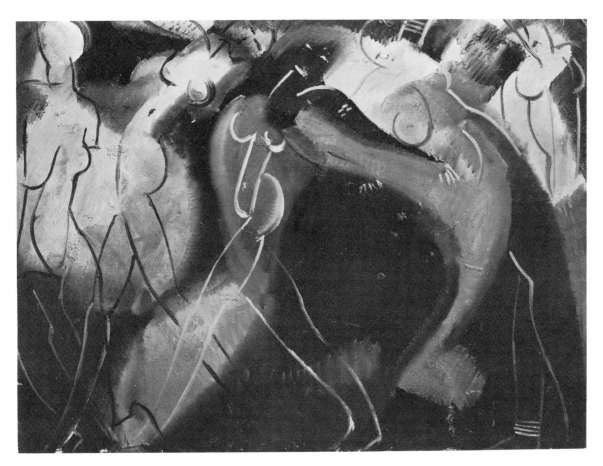

24 [10]

burgh, which included examples from all the regions of Scotland, Christian and non-Christian, of dates from the seventh to the tenth century A.D. The Celtic revivalists were more interested in the illuminated books of Kells and Durrow, which Johnstone got to know in due course. The quality he extracted from the disparate examples he was exposed to was just this 'rhythm'. Having isolated the quality to his own satisfaction he continued later, as a writer and teacher, to apply it as a yardstick to the most diverse art, from ancient Chinese bronzes to paintings of the School of Paris and the work of contemporary children. All this reflects the excitement of the twenties and thirties, when the liberating effect of modernism was opening up huge tracts of past and present art and artifacts to aesthetic appreciation, untroubled by overmuch scholarship or historical analysis. But it is not to say that Johnstone had not isolated an identifiable and valuable quality in his early Scottish sources. He was particularly stimulated by the rhythmic and repeated curve, whose most extreme form is the 'Celtic interlace'. Drawing on this basis does not easily serve the purpose of imitation; instead it has a natural dynamic and self-generating force. It is not a measured but an intuitive and compulsive way of proceeding. After the effect of cubism had been assimilated, interest in curvilinear rhythm revived. Particularly evident in the work of Miró, it was the only possible vocabulary for surrealist essays in automatism and impromptu composition. Later, Johnstone was to use it as a powerful aid in teaching drawing to children.

Johnstone sought to apply this curvilinear, rhythmic principle in a series of paintings that followed *Folies Bergères*. One lost picture, which was called *Rhythm* [*10*], came from two sources: underlying it is a pattern of light and shade deriving from his constant observation of cloud shadows moving over the border hills; superimposed on it is a rapid curvilinear drawing of nudes in motion, which owe their character to the five-minute life drawings he had to do in the Academie Colorossi. Images such as these nudes, however, became infrequent as Johnstone began to experiment with purely abstract expressions. He certainly painted some diverse works within a short space of time, but it is difficult to be sure how far these experiments could have been carried in the short time available to him at Selkirk. The picture now in the Scottish National Gallery of Modern Art, *Selkirk, summer, 1927* [*12*], named long after the event, is an example of a type he was then developing, but also of his habit of subsequent alteration. As it stands now, it is the product of two, if not three, distinct phases. The original curvilinear structure dating from 1927 can be seen in an early photograph [*11*]. The presence of the 'eyes' reminds us of the origin of this sort of thing in metamorphic imagery, and suggests, also, parallels with Picasso's contemporary paintings. Twenty years or more later, the bland shapes resulting from infilling between intersecting curves were tautened and toughened up, the eyes obliterated and a wiry structure of drawn lines superimposed over the whole. At this early period Johnstone was also experimenting with straight-edged

26 [II]

structures, but none as early as this survive [13].

These experiments eventually culminated in a series of paintings of surrealist character [18–21]; but before they emerged Johnstone's life had taken another decisive turn. After a year of painting in Selkirk, the Johnstones went on holiday – a painting holiday naturally – to Cagnes-sur-Mer. They had not been there long when news reached them that all Flora's money had been lost in the American depression. They were now on their own. Despondently they returned to Scotland, where William began to apply for teaching positions. He had no success, as his work entirely unfitted him for teaching, in the eyes of any Scots head teacher. They decided that the only thing to do was to seek work in America, in spite of the depression, as Flora's relatives and friends could perhaps help them. It seemed the last straw to John-stone's parents. But to America they went – to an America harder than it is today, but with undimmed zest and opportunity for excitement. After a series of casual jobs Johnstone found his feet – he was appointed lecturer in painting for one session at the California School of Arts and Crafts at Carmel. It is impossible to describe all the adventures of that time and the rugged, not to say frightening, characters he met there – like Mrs Amenta who controlled all the rackets in Monterey, and whose ambition was to learn to paint so that she could paint Jesus . . .; but these stories are best told by John-stone himself. He painted commissioned portraits in California, which have now been lost to sight; but surviv-ing photographs show that he was acquiring a good

mastery in portraiture, especially in a portrait of Flora's aunt, in which the powerful simplifications still show some application of Lhote's teaching [15]. Johnstone left many other paintings behind in California. Besides teaching at the School of Arts and Crafts, he had had private pupils; he and Flora had done decorative work for a new bank and had fought, almost literally, to get paid for it. They liked the country and things looked good. But money worries, homesickness perhaps, a rest-less search for his own tradition, were driving him home. Underlying all other causes was that deep-seated ten-dency of the man to withdraw from any situation that offered success at the price of definition. Was he beginning to take an American view, be accepted as American? Then he would assert his Scottishness. But he was deeply depressed when he had left behind the fruit-orchards of California for Glasgow in the rain and the sodden corn-stooks of a wet Scottish summer. They arrived back in Scotland in August 1929, with no change whatever in their real situation.

There followed nearly two more years of life when, whatever money or domestic worries he had, Johnstone was free to develop his painting. He began to pull together the experiments he had been making, keeping in mind the derivation from early British art but adding the influence of America and his awareness of what was happening in the world of art. To this time must belong, in origin if not always in completion, the series of paint-ings including *Germinal*, *Seed*, *Conception*, *Ode to the North Wind*, *Garden of the Hesperides* and, largest and

30 [*14, 15*]

most successful of them all, *A point in time*. These paintings present a puzzle historically speaking. Only in the most general sense can they be linked to the surrealist movement. In Europe, then, the choice for a young painter lay between surrealism and purist modernism represented by Ozenfant, Le Corbusier, and Mondrian. This latter had little appeal to Johnstone. On surrealism he was ambivalent, as nearly all British artists were. The induced paranoia and carefully fostered irrationality of surrealism were foreign to him, but he was in sympathy with its yielding to subconscious creative drives, its probing beneath the surface, its ambiguity and multiple imagery. The actual forms he used have an occasional suggestion of Tanguy or Arp and of a certain unusual kind of Léger, but they cannot be called derivative of any European surrealist. To anyone who knows how art feeds upon itself, and how extremely rare original imagery is, the paintings are intriguing, even baffling. However, the bafflement will only be increased if one insists on seeing William Johnstone only in European terms. The importance of America in his development cannot be exaggerated, and we must look there for any really close formal parallels to these early paintings. Certain paintings of Arthur Dove and Georgia O'Keeffe in the twenties and early thirties do provide such parallels, as Tamara Krikorian has already pointed out. In Georgia O'Keeffe's *Dark abstraction* of 1924 (St Louis), the quasi-organic swirling forms, with edges curving over, resemble Johnstone's *Conception* [*18*], while the same artist's *Black iris* of 1926 (Metropolitan

32 [17]

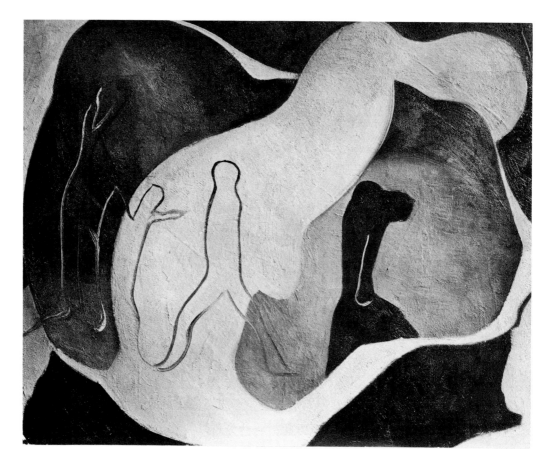

Museum) has a suggestion of deep cavities within a womb-like structure, also conveyed by *A point in time* [*21*] and other canvases of this group.

These analogies are close and striking, but it is by no means to say that Johnstone 'got it all' from O'Keeffe or Dove. The fame of these artists, who exhibited in Alfred Stieglitz's gallery in New York, was nothing then to what it is now. If Johnstone knew their work at all, it can only have been fleetingly in his passages through New York, and through occasional reproductions. Flora may have played a part in keeping him informed of what was going on in America, where native 'modern art' was only just then getting a toe-hold, although collectors like Barnes were buying extensively in Paris. Stieglitz's gallery would certainly have been an early port of call in New York for anyone interested in contemporary art in 1928 and 1929, as the Museum of Modern Art was not founded until late in 1929 (though preceded two years earlier by the 'Museum of Living Art' at New York University, now part of the collection of the Philadelphia Museum). Nevertheless, Johnstone does not recall going to the Stieglitz Gallery, of which he had never heard at that time.

Neither Arthur Dove nor Georgia O'Keeffe, nor yet William Johnstone – then or now – can easily be fitted to the standard structure of European art movements. With all these artists, we are surely dealing with a phenomenon more basic than any that can be comprehended in a single word like surrealism. We witness, in them, a revaluation of 'natural' art. They involve the painter not as observer, but as himself a part of nature. Their forms are organic and natural, but are used not to convey objective information, but to evoke feelings close to the psyche, sensations of existence in mind and body, time and space that the ordinary experience of 'nature' can no longer arouse. In O'Keeffe's paintings, the organic appearance conveys a powerful sexuality. In William Johnstone's paintings there are sub-aqueous depths and strange growths, ambiguous and metamorphic shapes, emergent forms glowing with colour, human forms merging one with another. The life of the paintings is barely controlled, and there is at that date no sense of the flat or the void as a positive good, a positive element in the balance of the painting. The curved line proves a fecund source of varied compositions, which are as spontaneous, and sometimes as artless, as those he later elicited from his pupils by teaching similar methods of composing. In pictures such as *Ode to the North Wind* [*19*], complex patterns of metamorphism and symbolism are set up, often of strongly sexual connotation, although not as overtly sexual as the forms of O'Keeffe. *Garden of the Hesperides* [*20*] has ghostly black-and-white female figures; *Ode to the North Wind* has interlocking forms of metamorphosed humanity, while in *A point in time* the forms are more generalised, with only a disturbing hint of organic growth going almost out of control.

A point in time [*21*], which must belong at least in its origin to 1929–30, is an astonishing achievement in every way. Nothing else like it could have been found in

36 [20]

Britain at that date. Its large size (also unusual for that date) draws in the spectator, in a manner not seen again until the 1950s, to float in zones of coloured light or probe deep cavernous spaces. But what is the underlying meaning of these paintings? Although Johnstone knew little of theoretical surrealism and could not have sub-scribed to its 'party line', they share with surrealism their fundamental motivation from the subconscious level, the level where all things are in flux, where eternity joins with the present in a condition of rolling change. Probably he never knew the words of A. N. Whitehead, which are so apt to his big picture: *a point in time is . . .*

the fringe of memory tinged with anticipation. Surrealism, too, dealt with the fringes of memory. Johnstone's memory held much that was revived in these paintings, just as his sensitive anticipation held much that was to come. They are documents of his inter-war years. They were also his principal expression until, years later, he developed a wholly different and more direct language of painting. But the period when he could develop these works in peace soon came to an end with the pressing need to launch out again and to earn a living. He had abandoned any hope of commercial success as an artist – his real paintings were unsaleable – and Scotland could offer him no teaching. At length, however, he managed to obtain a toe-hold in the metropolis.

Johnstone was taken on as art teacher in two boys' schools in north London in March 1931 at a salary of £180 a year. Since the work he showed at his interview was utterly unfamiliar to all concerned, he owed his appointment to the advocacy of R. R. Tomlinson, Chief Art Inspector for the L.C.C., who remained a firm supporter and friend. But meanwhile the situation looked grim: no more freedom but a great deal of exhausting work. Painting was at an end for the foreseeable future, for in order to make ends meet Johnstone was obliged to take evening classes as well for five nights a week. William and Flora had few possessions and found a room in Kilburn – hardly a bright district but better than the places where his schools lay. Faced with his classes, which included the usual proportion of hoodlums and boys who had nothing either to gain or lose, Johnstone knew that he was up against it. In this extremity, fortunately self-preservation and his own convictions pointed the same way. He was convinced of the vitalising force and absorbing interest of creative art, of the practice of art rightly taught. If he was right he could win the confidence of these children; if he was wrong he would go to the wall. He did prove the effectiveness of his methods, although he had a hard job bringing them to bear, harder perhaps in respect to headmasters and ministry inspectors, than in respect to the pupils. He began to acquire that capacity to deal with officialdom that took him to the top of the educational ladder, as well as the reputation as a disciplinarian for which he was famous, or somewhat notorious, at the Central School in later years.

In 1931, teaching of art in schools was hardly touched by modern influences. Meticulous copying, often from two-dimensional images, was still the rule. The grand debates of the nineteenth century about art education, centring on the problem of education for fine art versus education for design, had done little for the schools. There the debate was, or should have been, about art for children versus adult art imposed on them, or art as a creative outlet v .sus art as another form of authoritarian discipline. In this debate, 'Child Art' has won a great victory. The victory has been due in some measure to a tide of opinion outside the schools. Children's art has come up in the world, like primitive and ethnic art, in the wake of the modern movement, which has found the pure springs of art at deep-down levels in human development. But it has not been a one-way influence, and the pioneers of child art, that is pioneers in freeing the child to make his own art, were also contributors to the modern movement. In Johnstone's early days, there were little more than slight premonitions of all this. Non-authoritarian education was, in any form, an affair for foreigners and cranks. Among the foreigners were, of course, Froebel, Rudolf Steiner and, less well known, Frank Cizek (1865–1946), who ran an influential art class for children in Vienna from 1903 to 1938. Cizek's doctrine was the complete otherness of child art, and the weakness of his system was in its protectionism, the way he tried to stop adult influences reaching his pupils. Cizek's ideas were published or spread in this country by Marion Richardson, Francesca Wilson and William Viola, and it was the exhibitions organised by Marion Richardson that did most to alert the public to the real nature and the intrinsic attractions of 'Child Art'. Johnstone's appointment in 1931 must have been in part due to R. R. Tomlinson's early awareness of this new tide. Hardly any 'modern artist' had applied for teaching jobs before. Tomlinson told him that he 'had something greatly needed in London'. Perhaps unknown to himself, Johnstone became a pioneer of children's art education in London.

The foundation of Johnstone's teaching was simple: he believed in teaching as an artist teaching fellow-artists. This principle meant that his teaching practice was highly significant for his own work also. It was essential to his idea that pupils should find in themselves something to express and that even the most ham-handed of them should not be deterred by technical difficulties from doing so. No pupil should feel humiliated, so that none should be unwilling to contribute. The actual practice in class was founded in the development of scribbles, which yielded curvilinear shapes and rhythms analogous to those he had used in his own work. By careful selection and development with tracings, pupils developed their original scribbles into worlds of fantasy and imagination, or into abstract 'designs' often of much complexity and pictorial effect. Some extraordinary results obtained by this method are reproduced in Johnstone's book *Child Art to Man Art*, prepared in this period but not published until 1941. The reproductions show an intimate connection with Johnstone's own work – he was indeed teaching as an artist, almost as one of themselves. He freely says that he learned much from his pupils at this period. As the title of the book underlines, he differed radically from Cizek or those who inferred from him that 'child art' must be protected from adult influences, and stressed on the contrary that it must be used as the basis for growth into adult art.

R. R. Tomlinson took an acute interest in all this and defended Johnstone against unsympathetic heads and ministry inspectors who, when they came, reinforced his ready dislike for bureaucracy or pomposity. After a few terms Tomlinson decided that Johnstone ought to have a wider sphere to work in, and in 1932 he exchanged his badly paid full-time post for a better paid part-time one at Regent Street Polytechnic. There he encountered older pupils but also, what was to be very important to him, he widened his teaching to include day-release students and students of industrial design and architecture. With these pupils, he adopted the same basic methods but was able to extend them significantly into three-dimensional studies, the pupils practising the ready application of proportion, as music students practise runs and scales. After initial opposition his work was seen to be successful. Tomlinson then engineered his transfer to the Royal School of Needlework. To this appointment, William eventually added in 1936 the Headmastership of Hackney School of Art which was an evening institution. For the first time he could appoint his own staff, and his reputation for nosing out, or attracting into teaching highly talented but frequently eccentric artists, began to be established at that time.

These years, about 1935 to 1938, saw a steady improvement in William Johnstone's position, and it became possible to think again about his career as a painter, and developing his interests in other ways. His book *Child Art to Man Art* was on the stocks. As soon as he and Flora could get the time, they began to make expeditions to collect material for a book that had long been on his mind, which would express his ideas on the continuity of art in Britain. We have already seen how essential the linear basis of early British art was to Johnstone's own work. His book came out in 1936 under the title of *Creative Art in England*. An enlarged edition, including an account of the contemporary scene, was published in 1950 as *Creative Art in Britain* (considering that the jacket bore the famous Burghead bull slab from Moray, the change in title was timely). It is a highly personal and idiosyncratic book, not to be judged as history or scholarship, but perhaps unique in being a record, in a large number of plates, of what has moved an artist. Its content reflects all of Johnstone's predilections, with sympathetic perception of early art and few, perfunctory words about much else, the meat of the text being in the appendixes, where he reviews his ideas on basic training in art for children and students. As to Johnstone's painting at this time, there was no obvious change of direction, for the ideas and the actual paintings begun in Scotland still needed a great deal of development. So the late thirties was a time of consolidation in painting.

Naturally the Johnstones were not waiting on the sidelines for 'success' to come. Their life was an exceedingly busy one and brought them into contact with a large circle, including poets and musicians as well as painters and sculptors. If Johnstone ever had a 'group', it was the circle of Alfred Orage, editor of *The New English Weekly*. Through Orage he met Eliot, Pound, Dylan Thomas and Percy Wyndham Lewis. Lewis has remained for him the greatest English artist of the time, although their painting had nothing in common. Lewis's Vorticism had been forgotten and 'Modern Art' was still hardly known on the London scene. Johnstone's paintings were almost as far beyond most of the people he met in London, as they had been in Scotland. A very few galleries were then showing modern work: the Leicester Galleries; the Mayor, Zwemmer and Wertheim Galleries; the London Gallery, run by the Belgian E. L. T. Mesens, who had links with the surrealists; and one or two more. The Surrealist Exhibition in London in 1936 had included a section on British surrealists. Other configurations of British modernists were centred on the more formalist interests of *Unit One* and the periodicals *Axis* and *Circle*. Johnstone never appeared in any of these group contexts. The in-group, then as now, tended to dominate whatever activity there was on the London art scene. Johnstone was by background and inclination opposed to these groups, with their clubby and social overtones. But he began to appear in exhibitions from 1933, when he had some monoprints at the Mayor Gallery. His only one-man show up to the war was in 1935 at the Wertheim Gallery where Edward Marsh bought a painting – Johnstone's first recognition by the English ascendancy. This show was transferred to Aitken Dott, in Edinburgh, where it met with blank incomprehension.

In 1939 William Johnstone was included in two exhibitions which should firmly have established him in context – in the London Gallery in January–February 1939 he was in 'Living Art in England', a show including a large group of British modernists together with Gabo, Kokoschka and Mondrian who were by that time in England. In March he was in 'Abstract Paintings by Nine British Artists' at Reid and Lefevre, where McNeill Reid, son of the great Glasgow dealer Alexander Reid, was a friend and supporter. Paintings such as *A point in*

time, and others now destroyed, were shown in these exhibitions. Johnstone might have had a contract with Reid and Lefevre after the exhibition there; but he could not accept the limitations on his freedom that the gallery system would have imposed. Dealers have to interpret their artists to the buying public – they can recognise the aspects of an artist's work that may sell, and inevitably try to direct the artist towards those aspects. The more successful and established an artist is, the more freedom he can secure. But William, like many another artist since, jibbed at the idea that he might paint deliberately for sale. The quality of his refusal had, shall we say, a certain rigour that made a satisfactory relationship with dealers difficult if not impossible, then and after the war. For the 'successful' artist and influential critic, Johnstone has generally shown an implacable dislike. Interpret that how one will, it is by no means certain that he ever sought that kind of success for himself. He was incapable of ingratiating himself with the rich and influential; in many ways he was still a socially dissident Scot, who instinctively rejected and was rejected by the English ascendancy. He found the business of trying to interest dealers in his work baffling and distasteful. His friends were dissidents and radicals too. Flora was contemptuous of the bourgeois philistinism of London society. Johnstone was also a dissatisfied and perhaps confused romantic, who found it agreeable to believe, with Coomaraswamy and with more recent propagandists, that art should be ephemeral, done with as soon as painted. His enthusiasms had a childlike quality: they could be abruptly switched, and did not have a long-term objective goal. This sort of attitude was in the lifeblood of modern art, but the artists who changed the course of art most permanently were those who could project and externalise their own careers sufficiently to control their logical progression. Johnstone would, or could, never do this. But it was not until his post-war years that this failing, if it is one, acted seriously against his interests as an artist.

In 1938 Johnstone was appointed, against the odds, to the wholly full-time post of Principal of Camberwell School of Arts and Crafts, a school of 800 or 900 students. In September 1939 the outbreak of war crushed the infant growth of modern art in London and fastened this new responsibility about William's neck in a particularly burdensome way. Camberwell was in the most vulnerable area of all London, and Johnstone had to safeguard the School as far as possible and supervise its evacuation. Meanwhile he had a year of peace in which to make his mark at Camberwell. The methods he employed were founded on his past experience: bringing in enthusiastic staff who were artists primarily, trying to foster cross-fertilisation between departments, and constantly letting in the air of new ideas. He brought Victor Pasmore, who was then representative of the very best of the English tradition of sensitive, well-planned post-impressionism, and who while teaching in the painting school was able to consolidate the principles of the Euston Road school as a strong force in wartime and post-war painting. Johnstone's indifference to this kind of painting by no means prevented him from giving Pasmore his full support. Closer to his own interests were Norman Dawson and A. E. Halliwell, whom he appointed for their work with children and in basic design, respectively. Halliwell ran the Junior Art School and taught commercial design, including film animation, which Camberwell was the first school to teach. All this activity made Camberwell known far beyond its locality, and student applications increased. It made the School, under William Johnstone, a harbinger of post-war change. Time was to prove this, for Johnstone personally, a false dawn in some respects. Whatever may have been the case in other countries, in Britain there was and is no chance of founding a painting reputation on success in teaching, although the reverse may occasionally be the case. Even in the history of art education Johnstone has not had full credit for his innovations, a circumstance to which wartime upheaval, professional rivalry, and his own decisions all contribute.

The war of 1939–45 brought great changes to the lives of the Johnstones. The responsibility for a large London school under air attack took a serious toll on Johnstone. The junior schools of Camberwell, the Central School, and Hammersmith were all evacuated to Northampton, and had to be constantly visited, but the senior School remained although almost depleted of pupils. When things in Britain looked very grim, Flora and their young daughter went to America, and although they were out of the war they were the cause of greater anxiety to Johnstone than if they had remained

at home. Latent difficulties were exacerbated by distance, and eventually he learned that Flora was suing him for divorce. He was unable to get to the States to defend the action. These stresses broke Johnstone's health. He was absent from duty for almost a year, staying at Lockner Farm near Guildford, where he continued to live after he returned to work, travelling back and forth to Camberwell. He spent some part of his convalescence back in Scotland, and saw again the land he had left in order to follow the elusive hunt of art. When he was appointed Principal at Camberwell it had been hot news in Selkirk. But his father had only said 'no Johnstone has ever been a servant'. As he toiled about London among the bombs and the rockets, Johnstone must have thought it was servitude indeed.

During this crisis in his life Johnstone returned to painting. The paintings he produced at Lockner Farm were a new departure and marked the beginning of the gestural abstraction he has been known for since [24]. But even so they had a strong basis in experience, not only in the sombre colour with forms barely emerging from obscurity, which mirrored his state of mind at the time, but in a renewed interest in his home landscape. The Eildon Hills appeared again once or twice, and those rounded swelling hills lend themselves to metamorphic treatment, and merge easily into landscapes of the human body [22]. The wartime paintings are the pointers to the atmospheric and suggestive paintings of later years, where his whole life and emotions can be read if we can only lose ourselves in them. In *Nocturne*

[24] we may see both destructive fire, of which he had seen so much, but also a point of growth, a coiled bud of form ready to burst out. The paintings of this time also suffer from the historian's bane: they have mostly been altered when they have not been destroyed. It is hard to find works of earlier periods that have been sold straight off the easel and thus escaped later alteration. Johnstone sold little in this way and sales often went unrecorded. There are a few works very close to his heart that he never touched again, among them those of his family. The companionship of Mary Bonning, whom he had known as a student and met again in the darkest days, may literally have saved his life. They were married in 1944, and his paintings of her mark his emergence from despair [23]. Yet they do not attempt the delineation of character through the face, but only evoke a presence whose shape, as the light falls on it fitfully, is unmistakeably characteristic. From that time onwards, Johnstone has always chosen that way to evoke the people closest to him, culminating in his own recent series of self-portraits [48].

44

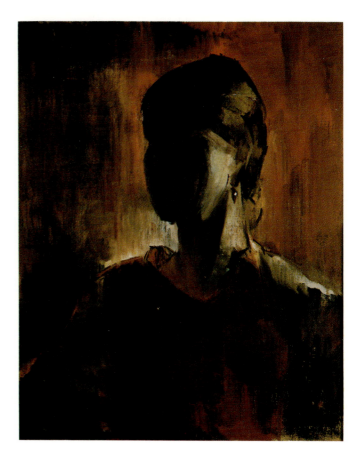

46 [*24*]

With his second marriage, the recovery of his health and the end of the war, a new chapter opened in the life of William Johnstone. The actual wartime paintings were naturally few. It was not until 1947 and 1948 that a corresponding new chapter in painting began. Johnstone's duties at Camberwell again absorbed him. There was a mood of post-war optimism among the ruins. Very many people turned to art in optimistic reaction to destruction. Government policy was to accommodate somehow the post-war thirst for more and better education. For a time the Camberwell School was almost a free-for-all, seething with students and returned staff, who included some of the most able artists in England, some of whom, like Lawrence Gowing, were shortly to take Camberwell ideas to new posts of influence elsewhere. Fundamental education was required for many of these students, so the conception of 'basic design' already mooted before the war, assumed a new importance. It was a time of new ideas in many directions and where new ideas come in, it is always a matter of politics, the manoeuvring of interests and personalities as the new beliefs and ideas jostle with the old. The politics of art education were part of a greater phenomenon, which might be called 'the coming of modern art to Britain'. To beleaguered Britain, 'abroad' seemed an immensely exciting idea; even France was accessible only with difficulty, but it was from Paris, inevitably, that the first wave of the ideological invasion came. The Picasso and Matisse exhibition, widely shown in 1947, was the first exposure to a British public of images that now seem classic, and provoked reactions recalling the best efforts of Edwardian philistinism. But this show was not the work of a private enthusiast like Roger Fry, but an early act of a powerful bureaucracy quite new to Britain.

Johnstone's attitude to this new art bureaucracy, which came to be concentrated in the twin powers of the Arts Council and the British Council, was always ambivalent to say the least. We will have to return to the subject, for it greatly affected his post-war career. Meanwhile the new movement had its effect closer home. The most distinguished painter on his staff, Victor Pasmore, adopted a new stance towards modernism in 1947. The London County Council, the senior governing body of the Camberwell School, did its bit in the new movement by organising the first open-air sculpture exhibition in Battersea Park in 1948, and it is difficult to exaggerate the importance of this series of exhibitions in the development of British sculpture. The idea of the exhibition was born in a suggestion by Johnstone to a member of the governing body. At just this time, the principalship of the Central School of Arts and Crafts fell vacant and Johnstone was invited, by a very narrow majority of the Governors, to take the post. It was the final sacrifice he made of his career as a painter to his career as an educator; he was now in one of the most senior art education posts in the whole country, and it made corresponding demands on him. Very remarkably – such was his amazing energy – his early years at the Central School were also productive years in painting. It was a conscious new beginning. He had accumulated large

50 [27]

numbers of paintings, thickly encrusted owing to his habit of painting over earlier work. Many had become cracked and damaged. In the awful winter of 1946–7, fuel was very short for heating water; there was a baby to be bathed . . . old paint burns very well. So we are lucky that some of the remarkably idiosyncratic work of the twenties and thirties does survive.

The painting of the late forties and early fifties reflects new interests. The revival of 'basic design' in the school, together with a revived interest in Poussin, was no doubt the source for a series of paintings incorporating spheres, cones and other regular shapes [30]. The curvilinear line of his pre-war compositions was replaced by a new form of drawing in sharp, energetic lines, hooks and dashes. This was a profound change. The new line did not generate illusions of organic forms in space, as the old line easily did. It was a much more direct, calligraphic or 'handwritten' expression of feeling. At the same time the misty suggestiveness of the few wartime pictures was carried over in pictures such as *Dark of the moon* [26] or the *Wapping* [27] series. Moreover, the quasi-organic forms of before the war had their counterpart in more wiry, bony, gnarled shapes. It is no use to consider these factors consecutively; they are all present in his work from 1947 to the middle fifties, and can even be seen together in the same picture. Johnstone was not settling down to produce pictures to demand, even his own demand. His canvases were arenas – a conception made familiar a few years later by the American exegesis of abstract expressionism, but unknown then. Any canvas may contain the record of several changes of mind, which could no doubt be painful, as they record not only interesting experimentation but hesitancy, self-doubt, self-scepticism and desire to change, conflicting with habitual practice. Plates [33] and [34] are a rare illustration of his method and of the difficulties in the way of chroniclers. Over a large canvas of unusually emphatic two-dimensional design, of uncertain date but highly effective character [33a], has been imposed a drawing whose relation to the design is obscure [33b]. That canvas was not taken further and still exists in the form shown. However, in another canvas of the same size the drawn design is worked out in the new misty, half-defined tonality [34].

All the different aspects are present in a large painting of the late forties, called *Sacred and profane love* [31] because its composition is said by Johnstone to be based on Titian's famous picture. The huge, knotty, branch-like forms that create two contrasting sides in the picture are defined by the new style of drawing, but their hardness is mitigated by modelling and shadows, to sustain the sense of ambiguity that Johnstone consciously or unconsciously always conveys. There is a photograph of this painting in a flat designed for the Hon. Gavin Astor by members of staff of the Central School, in the new idiom of *c*.1948 [p.86]. It is an interesting document, and seems somehow to symbolise Johnston's relationship and attitude at this date: he 'contributed a painting' and seems to claim no superiority for it over his staff's lamps and furniture. Indeed, design was then the main

54 [30]

preoccupation of the Central School and an area in which it scored some notable successes. As far as the School was concerned, Johnstone's painting was a private matter. Members of the staff who were painters hardly knew of it. Some of them were, or became while on the staff, far better known and commercially successful than he was.

William Johnstone's years at the Central School, from 1947 to 1960, were years of excitement, storm, stress, achievement and frustration. He inherited a school with great traditions, which had had on its staff men with household names, such as Bannister Fletcher, the architectural historian. It was largely the creation of W.R. Lethaby, the man who bridged the gap between William Morris and the modern world, and a spiritual parent of the Bauhaus. Johnstone was in complete sympathy with the aims of Lethaby and with the historic role of the School as one of the legs of a tripod on which art educa-

tion rested – the Central, the Slade and the Royal College, each with a different emphasis. He wanted to strengthen the role of the Central as a design school, not by narrow specialisation but by spreading creativity throughout the School as an underlying source uniting all technical disciplines. As at Camberwell, his appointments to the staff were brilliantly original. If there is one thing he is remembered for in that context, it was his appointment of 'fine' artists, young and intransigent, to long-established and 'safe' craft departments. Thus Eduardo Paolozzi was appointed to the textiles department, and Alan Davie to the jewellery department. The turn-over of staff was high. The list of staff who served under him is like a roll-call of the best-known names in post-war British art. But Johnstone is just as proud of the industrial brand-names that his students and staff made familiar in the shops and showrooms. Apart from this cross-fertilisation by staff, the main instrument in achieving the aim of unity was the 'basic design' concept, which was re-introduced from Camberwell. Johnstone strengthened the printing department, rightly sensing that using the alphabet is basic design training of the most effective kind. A. E. Halliwell was appointed head of a new School of Industrial Design. Later Victor Pasmore taught a wider Basic Design Course, and later still, after Pasmore had taken the concept to Newcastle,

William Turnbull strengthened it further. One of Pasmore's staff at Newcastle, Harry Thubron, set up a similar course at Leeds, so that from the parent course at the Central the 'basic design' concept achieved a wider circulation in the 1950s.

These developments in the hands of 'fine' artists were of great significance. They helped to shift the whole emphasis of advanced English art away from pictorial interpretation to expression by purely formal means. In this, of course, they pulled in the same direction as the modern movement as a whole, but the design-consciousness engendered by the English development left important aspects of modern art on one side and exposed much English painting to wearisome repeated accusations of prettiness and tastefulness. There is much debate about the pros and cons of 'basic design' in relation to recent English art (its effect in Scotland was much less); but it was a very important development and Johnstone has had no credit for his part in initiating it. He himself is partly to blame for that. Believing in basic design as primarily a discipline for designers, he was ambivalent in his attitude to it in painting. We have seen it reflected in work of his own, but thoroughly overlaid by elements of abstract expressionism. A more precise reason is his refusal to allow the Central School to take part in the first exhibition of the results of the basic design courses, *The Developing Process*, held at the ICA in 1959. He found some GLC regulation, prohibiting the removal of work from the School, to cover his decision, but the real reasons were surely personal ones, perhaps predominantly the feeling that he had lost control of something that had been 'taken up' by people who did not know their subject, and was becoming fashionable. It was an unfortunate decision to make, and it set him at loggerheads with many of the staff he had appointed, but it conforms to the pattern that he showed at other important moments in his life. It must be said that in spite of his refusal, his role in the development is clearly acknowledged in the catalogue.

58 [*33a*]

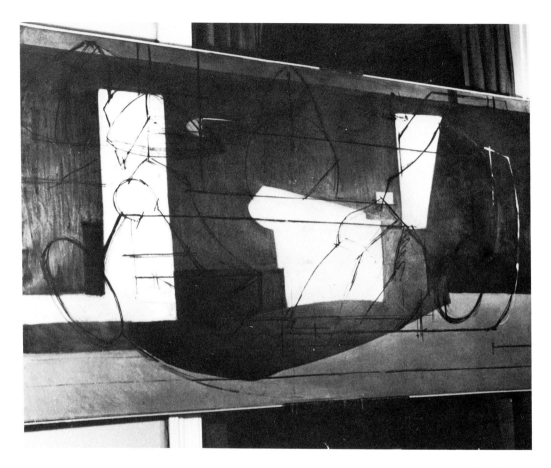

60 [*34*]

By 1959 Johnstone's own painting had changed again and had assumed fundamentally the character that it has today. The emphatically three-dimensional forms had dropped out, and line was no longer used anywhere to define boundaries. Coloured areas of dark, pungent intensity were allowed to make their own boundaries, their edges loose and dispersed like clouds or marked by vigorous strokes of the brush. Each of these areas has a spatial distance, the eye is still led into depth as it was in the previous pictures, the coloured areas interlock in three dimensions. Often this process is assisted by the most energetic lines drawn with a smaller brush, animating the structure of colours and sometimes hinting at different interpretations of the form. Where the painter chooses to emphasise the landscape origin, the brush lines may serve to show trees or hedges [37]. Elsewhere, over the sprawling form of a long hillside, say, there may be lines suggesting parallels between the hill and a recumbent figure [35]. Such paintings as Plate 29 seem very dense and richly worked today, when a thinner way of painting derived from American practice is much more familiar. Johnstone has always been very responsive to things American. His appreciation and understanding of the post-war American school is unusually deep, but it has had little effect on his own practice. Even his use of large canvases pre-dates their use by the New York School. If anything, his paintings of the fifties owe allegiance to the School of Paris, where from the early fifties *tachisme* was the dominant way of expression in abstract painting. The term defines a way of painting in which the brush stroke itself controlled, through the artist's spontaneous actions, the structure and development of the painting, invalidating pre-planning and defined boundaries. Johnstone's paintings conform to this type in general, but diverge from it when they are based too evidently on, say, a landscape structure.

The zenith of his *tachiste* work was in certain large canvases of the late fifties, which he was pleased to call *Northern Gothic* [40] because the late Daniel-Henry Kahnweiler, seeing one of them at the Lefevre Gallery, had speculated 'School of Paris ? But northern, perhaps Scandinavian ?'. These impressive works have a brush drawing of rugged, emphatic character, superimposed over blended colours full of light, air and distance, or over a white ground spattered with black. One of the finest of the series [41] is entirely monochromatic. These canvases hold a perfect balance between the form arrived at by and through colour, and the brush drawing, which too often in his work seems to have an obtrusive disconnected life of its own. Although they are wholly non-figurative, they are always redolent of the sensations of life – especially life under the elements, as he knew it so well. The great black brush-strokes fall across the canvas like the bitter squalls of early spring across the Border hills; like spring squalls they leave glimpses between them of memory and anticipation of light, warmth and growth. Jagged, fractured black forms stand out against watery white spaces like blackened thorns in winter against melting snow. Not all the *tachiste* pictures

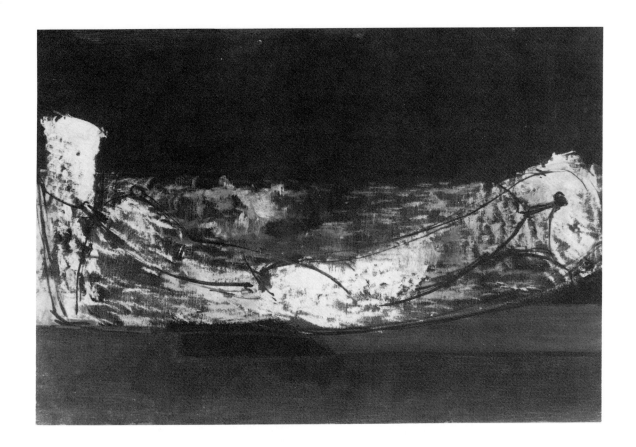

62 [*35*]

are as tough as this may suggest. This period also saw the beginning of the calligraphic brush-drawing, which later, in many works on paper, he raised to a more-than-oriental delicacy and subtlety [45]. Other paintings were again richly layered with contiguous slabs of colour, like adjacent fields of plough, grass and straw chequering the opposite hillside [36]. The fifties were a time of variety and achievement in painting. All the stranger that most of Johnstone's staff at the Central School hardly knew of him as a painter.

The year after his appointment to the Central Johnstone was able to revive a moribund fund in order to travel to the USA to study industrial design training. Again he felt the pull of America. Many of the great *emigrés* were still there in full career: he met Gropius, Breuer, Chermayeff – architects rather than painters, although he met Max Beckmann at Boston. When Frank Lloyd Wright suggested he stay on at Taliesin Johnstone was strongly tempted to accept. But in his absence unfortunate things were happening in London. Robin Darwin had been appointed Principal of the Royal College of Art, which was designed to become the prestige national art school (it eventually received university status). The Royal College was thus able to offer better salaries, and a large number of staff at the Central took advantage of their yearly contracts to transfer to the Royal College. Johnstone was furious, but soon came to realise that it provided him with opportunities for new and original appointments he would not have been able to make. But the incident, coming soon after his appointment, was unfortunately premonitory. That relations were bad between the Central and the Royal College did not matter so much – in a sense it concentrated his mind. He came to see the division between the two schools, and between himself and Robin Darwin personally, as symbolising something much deeper: the emergence in art education of that historic British fissure between the élite and the ordinary, the mandarins and the rest, the 'liberal' and 'mechanick' arts. Time was to prove him right, and the 'reforms' following the publication of the Coldstream and Summerson reports were to impose on the whole system a general theoreticisation and increase in regulatory bureaucracy.

Such ideas were gaining ground in the 1950s, and they were part and parcel of a similar process taking place at every level of the national apparatus for the support of art. Against this background Johnstone's decision to boycott the ICA exhibition is a little more understandable, and it is also the background to his activity as a painter who might have been, but was not, successful in the post-war world. This world was not exactly favourable to Johnstone's temperament and beliefs. Art students, as well as staff, were changing in character. The post-war bulge with its accompanying enthusiasm was waning. Perhaps in reaction to this, Johnstone became somewhat authoritarian in his approach – such, anyway, was his reputation. He found staff more difficult to deal with. Damaging rows occurred. All these things already inclined him to resign; meanwhile he had had since the early 50s a property again in the Borders, Ancrum Mill,

66 [38]

to which he came as often as possible. The pull of the Scottish land was again strong, and he exchanged Ancrum Mill for a larger farm. In 1960 he decided to offer his resignation from the Central School, and retired with his wife Mary, who threw herself energetically into the business of farming, and his young daughter Sarah to Satchells Farm near Lilliesleaf.

Like other moves in William Johnstone's life, this move expressed both an angry rejection of an aspect of life he did not like and an acceptance of his own nature. He heard his father's ghost speaking in the voice of the neighbour who came to urge him to buy Satchells. It was time to stop being a 'servant'. But we must also look again at what he was rejecting, and what he considered was rejecting him. How right was he, or how much was he bent on unnecessary self-destruction as a painter – a painter, that is, with some chance of success and renown? The briefest explanation is that he could not get on with the 'establishment' in art. It is true that such an establishment hardly existed when he first went to London. It grew up with the post-war growth of government funding of the arts, which required a class of officials and advisers to interpret the arts to government and distribute the money granted. Yet Johnstone had penetrated another sort of establishment, that of art education and the London County Council. And a powerful establishment it was, which brought him into contact with powerful men. Johnstone has no objection to power in itself. He describes with relish his encounters with these people, the battles of wits that sometimes resulted,

and his successes. (Was Johnstone the first to suggest to Sir Isaac Hayward that his memorial should be a great new gallery on the South Bank?) His troubles were with people of the mandarin class, and he could not judge fairly those fellow-artists he thought sucked up to them, played their game or learned their language.

The association of such a group of influential and sometimes wealthy intellectuals with contemporary art was something new. It marked the acceptance of modern art, not only as something worthy of private and public support, but as a fit subject for intellectual and scholarly study. This was possible for artists who took a more objectified and intellectualised view of their own art to accept, and to co-operate with. For artists like Johnstone, for whom painting was instinctive and very much his own business anyway, it was alienating. The situation was like a modern version of the old division already referred to between the liberal and the mechanical arts. Johnstone was by nature and conviction a 'mechanick'. He did not speak the language of the group who controlled the agencies of government support of the arts and exercised a powerful influence over the destinies of artists.

Johnstone faced this 'establishment' in two ways; as a painter and as an educator. As a painter he should have been in a strong position, for he was already a committed modernist. He did in fact have several post-war exhibitions; but he did not like the dealer system as it grew up after the war, and he never had the benefit of the thorough, professional promotion by a single gallery,

68 [*39*]

70 [41]

which was necessary. Some of his staff, who were then making names with the aid of the system, tried unsuccessfully to draw him into it. His rejection of these opportunities was a characteristic gesture of resistance. His hostility to the post-war élite was also sure to deny him success on this level. It leads him today to an assessment of the personalities involved – dealers, critics, artists – that is hardly fair.

As an educator Johnstone was also in a strong position as principal of the Central School. But the post-war reorganisation of art affairs could not be carried through and leave art education untouched. The alliance between scholarship and modernism, already referred to, was bound to promote the notion of the artist as an intellectual enquirer. This in turn led to a demand for the education of artists to have a more intellectual basis. The way this was carried through was profoundly worrying to one of Johnstone's views and he objected to what he regarded as the intrusion of gentlemen amateurs and the undue power they wielded through such bodies as the National Advisory Council on Art Education, chaired by William Coldstream. But before the Coldstream Report appeared in 1961, Johnstone had resigned from the Central School.

72 [42]

So William Johnstone became again a farmer. But although he had rejected the Central School and with it the 'art world' in which he had never been really at home, he did not reject painting. His compulsion to paint was equal to his compulsion to farm, and he was able to see both activities clearly (as he had always regarded them at heart) as coming from the same sources in the life cycle. He recognised himself as part of the cycle, through whom visual images pass 'almost without conscious intervention'. During the first few years at Satchells his split from the world of art was only relative. Many visitors from his old life came to stay there. As well as painting hard, he made an official visit to Israel in 1961 to report on art education there, and went to Paris with his friend McNeill Reid, who had also retired from London to live in Scotland. He had exhibitions at Graham Reid's Gallery in Cork Street in 1960 and 1964 and at the Stone Gallery in Newcastle in 1961 and 1963, which introduced him to a new circle of buyers.

But William and Mary decided to move again. They sold Satchells and moved in 1965 to Potburn, a great high stock-rearing farm at the head of the Ettrick Valley, in a very remote situation. There, things were much tougher. Unable to get into the farmhouse proper, the Johnstones rented a small house down the valley, Cossarshill, where there was little room to paint, and the presence of so many old canvases was oppressive. The number of visitors tailed off, as the place was extremely isolated. I went to Potburn in 1968 to choose a painting for the Scottish Arts Council, and later became a frequent visitor. Looking now to the past rather than the future, Johnstone was dictating his life story on to tapes. There were no more exhibitions with Graham Reid and the Stone Gallery. Characteristically, Johnstone permitted himself an exhibition, in 1969, at the short-lived Decor Gallery in Newcastle, run by a new friend and buyer, a wealthy young quarry-owner. It seemed a familiar sequence, with a maturing pattern of success disrupted by a new twist of escapism. In retrospect, the move to Potburn seems like the last of Johnstone's rejections, although it came out right in the end.

Several things conspired to turn Johnstone's thoughts to painting and the future again. The purchase for the Scottish Arts Council was followed by one for the Scottish National Gallery of Modern Art in 1969, and the promise of a retrospective exhibition in the new Arts Council gallery in Edinburgh, which took place in 1970. These events made him feel the possibility of acceptance as a painter in Scotland. In 1969 Johnstone met Mrs Hope Montagu Douglas Scott, his contemporary, who became a friend and a patron of a generosity rare today, and of incalculable value to a painter experiencing a renaissance of late life. Warned by illness that his days as an active farmer were over, and knowing that his wife and daughter could not go on shouldering an increasing burden of large-scale farming, Johnstone sold Potburn in 1970 and retired to Palace, a Victorian house with a few acres in the Teviot Valley near Crailing, a gentler, more accessible place. Here he had all the room he wanted to paint, draw and review the work of a lifetime.

He was seventy-three, but he was about to enter on the most productive decade of his life. He was able to cultivate old and new friendships, comment with wry trenchancy on events in the world of art and farming, continue to polish his autobiography, star in two films, and see the trickle of people who were now interesting themselves in his work.

Johnstone had painted a few pictures at Cossarshill, expressive of his sombre mood at that time. A short sequence entitled *Rain in Ettrick* [43] revives the feeling of his wartime pictures at Lockner Farm. On settling at Palace, he could for the first time think of improving his technical resources. The small brush drawings he had made all through the late fifties and sixties now increased in size, aided by an adjustable table that allowed him to control the fall of the ink or watercolour. He was able to embark on large canvases again. A new venture was a series of reliefs in plaster. The central theme and controlling character of all the work of the seventies is a new urgency in respect to time, and a new interest in fate or chance. He was fond of quoting Burns on poetic creation: 'but how the subject-theme may gang, let time and chance determine. Perhaps it may turn out a sang, perhaps turn out a sermon'. It is an exhausting method for a painter in his seventies, involving occasional bursts of activity at full stretch, between longer spells of passivity. Like the surrealists at the time of their experiments in automatism, Johnstone has tried to make himself no more than an outlet for impulses from within and outside, associating himself in a pantheist way with all nature. This was not a new idea, for he was aware of the surrealists' theories on automatism as far back as the twenties. But he had greatly refined his means and brought a lifetime's experience of the workings of time and chance to these last works.

The most typical expression of the period are the ink drawings, which touch the deepest aesthetic nerve. The black stroke on dazzling white means instant success or failure in aesthetic terms, as the eye responds first to the quality of the gesture that made it, the way it is started, carried through and terminated, then to its material appearance, its transparency, solidity, sharpness and softness of edge; then to the interval between it and the next stroke, their relationship to the empty paper and its edges; and finally assesses the symbolic content of the whole. In painting it is necessarily more complex – Johnstone's attempts to paint large unified gestural paintings analogous to the drawings have not been so successful. The best of his late large canvases, *Celebration of earth, air, fire and water* [44] and *Resurgence* are successors to the *Northern Gothic* series, but are at the same time more urgent, more questioning, and more contemplative. Their calligraphy is less emphatic, their zones of colour more suggestive. In an indefinable way they are richer and deeper.

The series of plaster reliefs is perhaps incidental to Johnstone's main work but because of the nature of the medium it illustrates his ideas of time and chance better than any other work. Briefly, the idea behind the series is to set a limit on the time available to him to make an

76 [44]

effective creative gesture. A helper stands by with wet plaster and places lumps of it on a board to the direction of Johnstone, who, trowel in each hand, drags and twists it as he might draw ink with a brush. He had a few minutes while the plaster remained manipulable in this way. The result was to isolate a small number of basic forms and actions in his repertory, and to throw up some felicitous results. It was very far from the nature of relief as a separate medium and did not add significantly to his range of expression, but these plasters highlighted for Johnstone both the fragility of the creative impulse and its forcefulness when it comes, its capacity to drive through the heavy crust of earthy material – 'the force that through the green fuse drives the flower'. For that reason he called the whole series *Genesis* [*46*].

Another separate effort in the seventies was his series of lithographs made to accompany poems by Hugh MacDiarmid, a return tribute, forty years on, to the verses MacDiarmid had written to Johnstone's paintings in 1933, which had only been published thirty years later. These lithographs posed a fascinating technical problem to Johnstone in the translation to a new medium of his ideas of growth and chance, but they cannot be considered stylistically separate from his contemporary drawings. With the collaboration of Kenneth Duffy of the Printmakers Workshop in Edinburgh, James Gardiner the designer and Fiona Campbell the binder, the lithographs and poems were made up into a superb *beau livre* of a kind rarely produced in Britain, and were launched at an exhibition at the Printmakers Workshop

Gallery in 1977. The decade began with the retrospective exhibition at the Scottish Arts Council Gallery in 1970, the first time the painter had been required to step back and see his work as a whole, and attempt to establish its chronology. There were exhibitions at the MacRobert Centre of the University of Stirling in 1972 and 1974, at the Scottish National Gallery of Modern Art in 1973 (of the plaster reliefs only), at the Talbot Rice Art Centre in the University of Edinburgh in 1976, and at the Third Eye Centre in Glasgow in 1977. At the time of writing, a retrospective exhibition is planned for the Hayward Gallery in 1981.

If William Johnstone exhibits at the Hayward in 1981, it will be another complete turn of the wheel of life, just twenty-one years after he left the London scene for good, as he thought. In the space of a long life, he has fulfilled two cycles, as farmer and artist, each of which he had at one time rejected for the other. And this fulfilment has brought to the one-time rebel and maverick a rare maturity in all things that concern art and life. For Johnstone, art is so interwoven with life that it can hardly be extricated as a separate object of study. Instead of asking 'what sort of painter is William Johnstone?' one is forced to ask 'what sort of man?' And the answer does not come readily, for his character is elusive and complex. Drawing on our many conversations, and on many pages of autobiography as yet unpublished, I have tried to trace influences and events that moulded it, and how he also moulded those things and people round him. It is time to attempt a summing up of a kind.

Johnstone is a free spirit to an unusual, enviable degree. He has paid a high price for freedom, not merely the eternal vigilance it is said to depend on, but an eternal resistance to absorption. To some extent he was unable to help himself, for somewhere within this resistance was the painful diffidence of the Scot, who veers so easily between humility and arrogance and does not recommend himself by either to his English neighbours. Be this as it may, to keep aloof from the collective enterprises of post-war painting, never to have associates in painting with whom to discuss one's work, this was a high price to pay for freedom – indeed a deprivation. But consider the alternative. If William Johnstone had played all the right cards, he might have been among the first dozen names in modern British art. But he would never have completed his second cycle, and he would probably not be enjoying an extraordinary late flowering or be, so radiantly, a free man who has never compromised with anybody. Had he chosen to pursue success as a painter, his role in art education would have been less dynamic, and the careers of several younger stars of post-war British art would have been different, and their trajectories perhaps less brilliant.

As it is, Johnstone is remembered with gratitude as the animator, *par excellence*, of post-war art education. His staff remember him as authoritarian, hard on weakness, respecting spirit, but above all mindful of their, and his, position as artists and invariably willing to help them

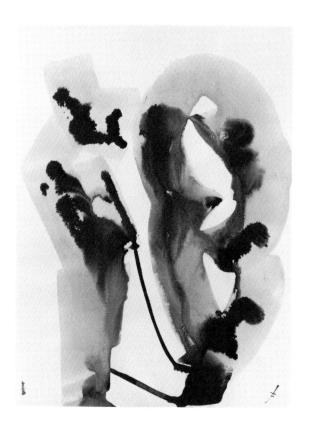

when those interests were at stake. A real, modern artist-principal was a rare and valuable thing, although later staff, at the Central, might have known nothing of his work. There seems to have been a difference in this respect between staff nearer his own age, whom he could regard as sharing an adventure with him, such as Hans Tisdall and Victor Pasmore, and the younger staff who came later to the Central. Some of his most successful relationships were with men who taught in the design departments, and who were inspired by the way Johnstone was able to relate the growth of industrial design to the older arts and crafts traditions of the Central School, his application to it of a sense of abstract poetry, and his desire to bring all the teaching together as only different aspects of creative thinking.

As a painter, Johnstone was fortunate to be born into the twentieth century. Only in recent times could the qualities of his mind and imagination have found such a direct expression in his work. The idea of painting as a sort of writing on canvas wherein may be read the state of the artist's soul, and through him the state of the world – that idea was not new when Johnstone painted his first gestural or *tachiste* canvases in the 1950s. He has remained faithful to it, however, after such painting has largely passed into history. Even his earlier painting prefigured it, and today only such painting can properly express his inner character. Each time he faces a blank canvas or sheet of white paper, he re-enacts the drama of the young man making his first moves in life . . . instinct with life. His feeling for life does not find an

outlet in deliberate representation: it fills each stroke with representational, or rather *representative* meaning. The development of a painting or drawing thus becomes charged with multiple values. The first dense vertical stroke may well symbolise integral man: the first horizontal one his environment. These first steps in the development also establish the white ground as a screen whereon energy is recorded, and a social frame wherein a system of relations is set up and elaborated. But not too elaborated: often, in drawing, a few strokes suffice to indicate the complete picture, and this is welcome to Johnstone, for success with the simplest means is a high order of success to him. But the system is capable of infinite elaboration, as he strives to express his sense of continual change, of all things being a continuum; as physical involvement with the management of the painting raises interest to the level of passion; as a sense of tragedy or achievement or hope comes up from underneath and becomes the dominant motive of the whole work. These experiences cannot be planned, they are instinct and intuition made visible. Nor can the works these experiences produce be satisfactorily analysed.

To some of Johnstone's staff at Camberwell and the Central, and others in other walks of life who have encountered him, he has seemed a dreamer and a mystic. In earlier life such an impression was offset by an intense practicality. But in later life, he is able to dream and, in the manner of old men, to review his past life. Does he regret the twists and turns, the evasion of his career, his refusal to come to terms with the society he found himself in at various times and to use the openings it offered? Does he regret the half-acceptance of his fate as a painter, the postponement of his creative crisis through his involvement with art teaching and other things, so that this crisis came so late, and in a diffused manner? By creative crisis I mean the time when an artist comes to terms with his real nature and powers and the extent of his understanding of art, with a knowledge of what has been done and also what must still be done – if indeed he has the capacity for this self-knowledge. Looking at the ripe, comfortable and productive old age that William Johnstone now enjoys, one must think that there is little to regret, that all cycles are now complete. His pantheistic philosophy informs his age; his grief for a world that rejects his values has quite swallowed up his private regrets. He says: 'in another life I would not be an artist, I would choose to spend my life studying the behaviour of animals'. Now he has opportunity to do that, and to contemplate the cycles great and small, of the life and death of snow flakes, petals, cattle, farms, men. But, reluctantly or gladly, the sap still rising in him, he goes back to his studio. It is for us to accept his life work as the fruits of one of nature's cycles and enjoy it.

Select Bibliography

WRITINGS BY WILLIAM JOHNSTONE

Creative Art in England. Stanley Nott 1936.

'The Impersonal in Classic Art', *Art and Education* 6 (December 1939).

Child Art to Man Art, Macmillan 1941.

'The Education of the Artist', *Studio*, vol.124 (January 1943).

Conception, designed and printed at Camberwell School of Arts and Crafts 1939–47 (book of reproductions, including three works by W.J.).

'Unity of Art and Industry', *Times Review of Industry* (December 1948).

Creative Art in Britain, Macmillan 1950 (enlarged edition of *Creative Art in England*).

'Graphic Design at the Central School', *Penrose Annual*, vol.47 (1953).

WRITINGS ON WILLIAM JOHNSTONE

A. T. Cunninghame 'William Johnstone', *Studio*, vol.124 (January 1943) 13–14.

Denis Saurat 'Scottish Intellectualism: William Johnstone', *Studio*, vol.124 (August 1943) 54–5.

M. Bernd-Cohen 'Portrait of the Artist', *Art News and Review* (7 March 1953).

Patrick Heron 'Notes on Nine British Artists', *Arts Digest* (15 March 1955).

Anton Ehrenzweig 'William Johnstone, Artist and Art Educator', *Studio*, vol.157 (May 1959) 146–8.

A. Ehrenzweig *William Johnstone*, printed at the Central School of Arts and Crafts, n.d. (1959). An enlarged version of the preceding text.

Tamara Krikorian and John McEwen 'William Johnstone, a Survey', *Studio International*, vol.189 (March/April 1975) 88–92.

POEMS BY HUGH MACDIARMID

Poems to paintings by William Johnstone, written *c*.1933, first published by K. D. Duval, 1963; reprinted in *The Complete Poems of Hugh MacDiarmid*, vol.11, Martin Brian and O'Keeffe 1978. The titles are: A Point in Time; Wedding of the Winds; Conception; Composition; Knight; Of William Johnstone's Art; Ode to the North Wind; Of William Johnstone's Exhibition (some of the last poem was incorporated in a poem of 1956, *Artistic Development in Scotland*, first published in the Complete Poems, 11, pp.1398–9.

The above list does not include exhibition reviews, which are numerous.

One-man Exhibitions

1935 May–June: Wertheim Gallery, London
1935 October: Aitken Dott & Son, Edinburgh
1950 June: Colorado Springs Fine Art Center
1953 March: The Lefevre Gallery, London
1958 January–February: The Lefevre Gallery, London
1958 December: The Bear Lane Gallery, Oxford
1960 November–December: The Reid Gallery, London
1961 September–October: The Stone Gallery, Newcastle
1963 August–September: The Stone Gallery, Newcastle
1964 October–November: The Reid Gallery, London
1969 October: The Decor Gallery, Newcastle
1970 July: Scottish Arts Council, Retrospective Exhibition, shown in Edinburgh, Aberdeen, Glasgow, and the Morley Gallery, London
1970 July: Great King Street Gallery, Edinburgh
1970 November–December: Compass Gallery, Glasgow
1973 June–July: Scottish National Gallery of Modern Art, Edinburgh
1974 April–May: MacRobert Centre Art Gallery, Stirling
1976 August–September: Talbot Rice Art Centre, Edinburgh
1977 August: Print-makers Workshop Gallery, Edinburgh
1977 August–September: Third Eye Centre, Glasgow

Selected Group Exhibitions

1935 August: 'Contemporary Scottish Painting', The Gallery, St Andrews
1939 January–February: 'Living Art in England', The London Gallery
1939 March: 'Abstract Paintings by Nine British Artists', The Lefevre Gallery, London
1949 November: 'William Johnstone, Jean Lurcat, William Gear', Gimpel Fils, London
1977 August–September: 'Painters in Parallel', Edinburgh College of Art

Greenhead Farm, Selkirk (see p.1)

List of Illustrations

Unless otherwise stated, works are in the possession of the artist's family. The publishers are grateful to those individuals and institutions listed below for permission to reproduce work in their possession. Dimensions are given in millimetres and inches, height before width. Unless indicated otherwise, the works are in oil.

The Hon. Gavin Astor's flat (see p.52)